shih tzu

understanding and
caring for your dog

Written by
Pat Lord

shih tzu

understanding and caring for your dog

Written by
Pat Lord

pet book publishing

Pet Book Publishing Company

The Old Hen House, St Martin's Farm, Zeals, Warminster,
Wiltshire, United Kingdom BA12 6NZ

Printed by Printworks Global Ltd., London & Hong Kong

Every reasonable care has been taken in the compilation of this
publication. The Publisher and Author cannot accept liability for any loss,
damage, injury or death resulting from the keeping of Shih Tzu by user(s)
of this publication, or from the use of any materials, equipment, methods
or information recommended in this publication or from any errors or
omissions that may be found in the text of this publication or that may
occur at a future date, except as expressly provided by law.

The 'he' pronoun is used throughout this book instead of the rather
impersonal 'it', however no gender bias is intended.

ISBN: 978-1-906305-64-2

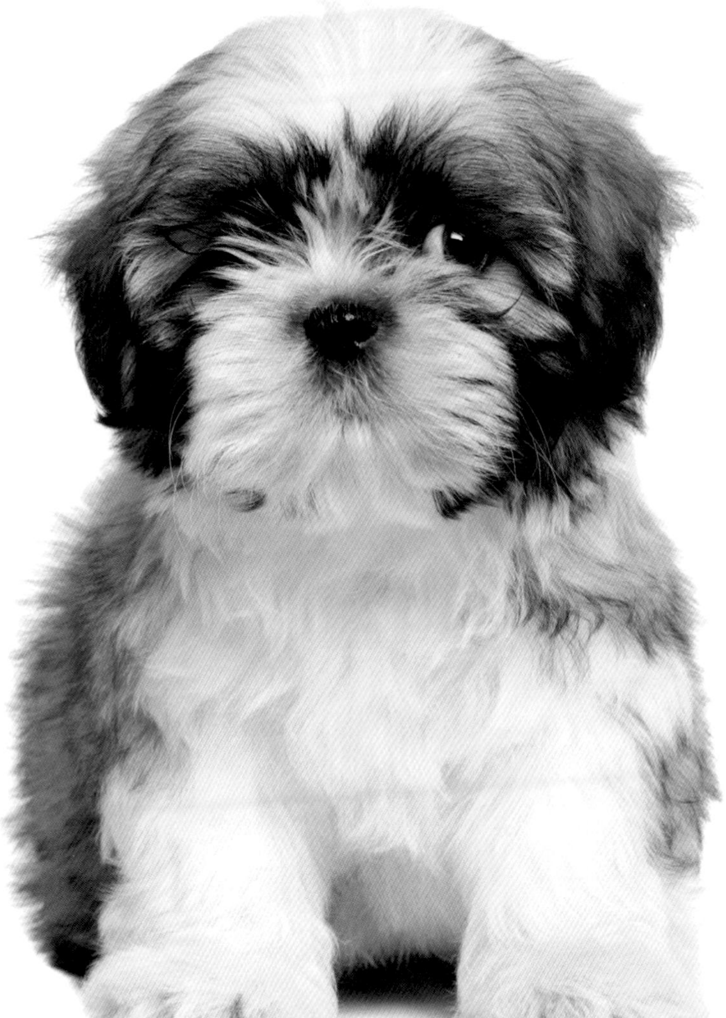

Contents

Introducing the Shih Tzu

Although this breed is presented in a small package, the Shih Tzu considers himself to be a big dog. With his superb temperament, character, and good looks, it is easy to understand how this little dog can steal your heart away.

The Shih Tzu (pronounced Sheed Zoo) was bred primarily as a companion, and you could not wish for a better friend and playmate. He is so adaptable, suited to the town or country, prepared to rest quietly by your chair, romp in the garden, or enjoy long country walks. A close friend thought I was somewhat eccentric when I referred to one of my Shih Tzu as a "little person" – that is, until the lady in question owned one! The Shih Tzu is so humanized it is astonishing and, for me and many others who have the pleasure of owning this little dog, there is no better companion.

Here we have a breed, thankfully, born without many health problems, but it is not the dog of choice for everyone. The Shih Tzu has a long coat, which looks stunning when it is properly cared for, but this demands a huge amount of time and commitment, unless you opt to keep your dog in a pet trim. Even so, this is not a breed for someone who wants to cut corners with coat care. The Shih Tzu coat requires daily attention, and grooming your dog needs to be an established – and enjoyable – part of your day.

The Shih Tzu thrives on company, and he will pine if he is left for long periods on his own. He is certainly not suited to outdoor housing. He is a happy, endearing companion, and although easy to train, he has a mind of his own.

We are lucky that the Shih Tzu is a relatively long-lived breed, and, with luck, will live well into double figures.

The Shih Tzu temperament

First and foremost, the Shih Tzu adores people; he has the knack of being very attentive without being too fussy or demanding. He is good with children, and will be more than happy to join in with their games. He is alert but certainly not yappy, as he is far too intelligent to waste time and energy on unnecessary barking. He gets on well with other dogs and animals of all sizes; Shih Tzu also have an uncanny ability to recognise their own breed. Once you own one, you will find it a great temptation to make it two!

The Shih Tzu is an active dog that loves to play, especially with soft toys. The independent streak means he can amuse himself for hours with dog toys – or sleep happily in the security of his own home.

In terms of exercise, the adaptable Shih Tzu will enjoy whatever he is given.

Tracing back in time

We are able to trace back, for hundreds of years, to a small dog resembling the Shih Tzu that was bred in China. However, it is believed that the breed originated in Tibet.

Known as Tibetan Lion Dogs, these little dogs were considered sacred in Buddhism, and were specifically bred by Chinese eunuchs and Tibetan monks to resemble the lion.

There are ancient scrolls depicting pictures of these 'lion dogs', also known as Foo Dogs; the male is often shown with his front foot on a ball. Statues of these holy dogs were placed to guard the entrance to Buddhist temples.

The Shih Tzu bears a resemblance to the other Tibetan breeds, namely the Lhasa Apso, Tibetan Terrier, and Tibetan Spaniel, which leads some historians to believe they are related.

However, others consider that the Shih Tzu is more likely to have been crossed with the other short-faced oriental breeds, such as the Pekingese, Pug and Japanese Chin.

Whatever we are led to believe, these little lion dogs were highly prized and are an integral part of Chinese history, tracing back as far as the Ching Dynasty in 1644.

The most famous kennel in China was that of the Dowager Empress Cixi, who bred Pekingese, Pugs and Shih Tzu, but after her death in 1908 the kennel was disbanded. The breed became extinct in China after the Communist Revolution of 1949.

Coming west

Luckily, diplomats who had been stationed in China, brought home several Shih Tzu and the breed started to become established in Europe. These dogs included three imported by Lady Brownrigg in England for her Taishan kennel, and six other imports which came into England between 1933 and 1959.

British foundation stock included two additional dogs, Aidzo and Leidza, who were both given to the Queen Mother in 1933. These dogs came from Mrs Henrik Kauffman of Denmark, although they were both born in Beijing.

In the early days in England, the breed was known as Tibetan Lion Dogs and even classed as the same breed as the Lhasa Apso and shown alongside it. In 1934 the Tibetan Breed Association stated that the Tibetan Lion Dogs were a separate breed, and this is when their name was changed to Shih Tzu, which was how they were originally known in China.

Below: The Lhasa Apso bears a strong resemblance to the Shih Tzu.

Developing the breed

The Shih Tzu increased in popularity in England and by 1939, 183 Shih Tzu were registered with the English Kennel Club, and by 1940 Championship Show status was granted.

However, during World War Two breeding virtually came to a standstill. From l945 the registrations slowly began to increase and the first Champion, Ta-Chi of Taishan, was made up in 1949.

When the Shih Tzu was first imported into America in the late 1930s, there were similar problems with establishing its identity; it was not recognized by the American Kennel Club (AKC) as a separate breed. At that time, the majority of the imports were made by army personnel who had come across the breed whilst stationed in England or Scandinavia. The breed was shown and bred as Lhasa Apsos, until the Shih Tzu became officially recognized by the AKC in 1955.

The first purebred Shih Tzu to be imported into America, registered, and recognized as a separate breed, was a bitch from England, Golden S Wen of Chasmu. She was imported by Maureen Murdock and her nephew, Philip Price.

Philip Price went on to breed from this imported bitch and exhibited the first Shih Tzu in 1957, in Philadelphia. The breed was then shown for the first time at Westminster Show in 1961.

The Pekingese cross

In the UK, the post-war recovery of the breed soon met with problems. There were those who considered that the Shih Tzu was becoming too big, and that there were too many faults creeping in. It was felt the breed would benefit from being crossed with the Pekingese.

In fact, the cross between these two breeds was to cause considerable controversy, not only at the time but for many years following.

Miss. E.M. Evans, a Pekingese breeder, mated the two breeds in an effort to reduce size, length of leg and improve pigment – but we must bear in mind that the Pekingese, at that time, were quite different in stature to those of the present day. Permission was granted by the Kennel Club for the fourth generation of the cross to be registered as purebred Shih Tzu.

Facing Page:
Controversy was sparked when the Shih Tzu was crossed with the Pekingese.

Further trouble was to come as the established Lhakang kennel started to breed tiny Shih Tzu; this was considered by many to be most detrimental to the breed, causing difficulties in whelping. Although classes were put on at dog shows to accommodate smaller dogs, after various meetings the Breed Standard was changed to a minimum limit of 10-18lb (4.5-8kg), an ideal of 10-16lb (4.5-7.5kg).

Worldwide favorite

Regardless of controversy within the breed, numbers were increasing and a further club, the Manchu Shih Tzu Club, was formed in 1958. By 1970 there were numerous exports, mainly to the US, and by 1980 the registrations had reached into the thousands, with six breed clubs in the UK.

In the USA, the development of the Shih Tzu can be attributed to the enthusiasm and knowledge of Ingrid Colwell.

She moved to America from Sweden with her American husband, taking with her five purebred Shih Tzu. These dogs included French Ch. Jungafelts Jung-Wu and two with the Pukedals affix, who had been bred by Ingrid's mother in Sweden.

Ingrid imported several more Shih Tzu from England and Scandinavia, and, in total, bred 79 Shih Tzu before her untimely death in a fire. As the Shih Tzu gained rapid popularity, the AKC opened its Stud Book to the breed in March 1969. Nowadays the breed registration in America is close to 4,500 per year.

In the UK, the Shih Tzu gained considerable popularity in the 1990s, and competition in the show ring became very strong, with huge numbers of entries and the presentation of the dogs improving all the time.

Over the next few years dogs were imported through quarantine from various countries, including Norway Sweden, Germany and USA, as at it was considered by some that the breed needed to increase its gene pool.

The new stock was imported with the aim of combining it with the best English dogs to improve and strengthen the breed, particularly in relation to pigmentation, color, conformation and style.

It is now firmly established as a glamorous show dog, and an outstanding companion dog on both sides of the Atlantic.

What should a Shih Tzu look like?

The Breed Standard is a written blueprint, describing not only the physical appearance, but also the ideal temperament and characteristics essential to a particular breed.

Every pedigree dog has a Breed Standard to adhere to, which is drawn up by breed clubs and authorised by national Kennel Clubs. The aim is to give guidance on the essentials of the breed, and to protect it from exaggerations, which could be detrimental to the health of the animal.

Although the Breed Standard for the Shih Tzu, both American and English, describe the same breed of dog, there are a few interesting written differences between the two official Breed Standards, which are noted below. In America the Shih Tzu is shown in the Toy Group whereas in England the breed is shown in the Utility Group.

General appearance

The Breed Standard starts with an overall impression of the breed – but there is an important factor to consider. The Breed Standard has been written for a Shih Tzu that is in coat, i.e. not clipped or trimmed in anyway. Clipping or trimming is not allowed by Kennel Club rules if the dog is to be exhibited in the show ring.

As you will see from the many photographs featured in this book, there is a significant

difference in general appearance between a dog in full coat and those that have been clipped or trimmed – although we are dealing with the same dog 'underneath'. The Breed Standard asks for a "sturdy dog", by this it means carrying a good weight and having substance. An abundant, but not excessive, coat is asked for, and the dog should carry himself with an air of arrogance. The chrysanthemum-like face is a feature of the breed.

Well, yes, the Shih Tzu certainly has a proud demeanor with a sense of importance which could be called arrogant. The chrysanthemum-like face is easy to envisage if you imagine the biggest bloom you have ever seen on a chrysanthemum, with each petal delicately folded into one another. This depicts the glorious round head of a Shih Tzu – covered in luxurious head hair, which you can cup gently between your hands.

Temperament

The Shih Tzu is described as being intelligent, active and alert, with a friendly and independent temperament. This sums up the endearing small size, 'huge heart', little dog. You will find that the Shih Tzu simply overflows with character and intelligence – in fact, he is usually one step ahead of you.

Head and skull

The head is described as broad and the top of the skull is quite round. As the Shih Tzu grows from a puppy, so does the coat, the beard and the whiskers – the hair growing upwards and outwards from the muzzle. This hair growth helps to give the distinct 'chrysanthemum-like' affect.

The Shih Tzu is intelligent and friendly with a notorious independent streak!

This is particularly striking in youngsters, before the hair becomes too heavy and needs to be tied up. Obviously, this hair growth should not allow the dog's eyes to be damaged or affected in anyway.

The muzzle should be of ample width, square and short; it should be flat and hairy with no evidence of wrinkles. The width and padding of the muzzle can make a vast difference to the soft expression required by the Breed Standard.

The Shih Tzu's delightful nose should be black, but dark liver in liver or liver-marked dogs is permissible.

The length of the nose should be about one inch (2.5cm) from tip to the definite stop between the eyes. The nose is required to be level, but a slightly tip-tilted nose is allowed which gives a more oriental expression. Wide open nostrils are asked for to help to avoid breathing problems.

Down-pointed noses are highly undesirable, as are pinched/tight nostrils. The Breed Standard states that pigmentation of the muzzle should be as unbroken as possible.

Eyes

Large, dark, round eyes are asked for, placed well apart with a warm expression. I cannot emphasise enough how essential it is to have correct eyes. To look into the correct dark eyes of a Shih Tzu is to see the entire appeal of the dog. Their warm, trusting expression can make you glow, even on a cold, damp day!

The eyes should not be so large as to be prominent, or bulbous, as they could be easily damaged if this was the case. Lighter colored eyes are only permitted in liver or liver marked dogs, and no white of eye should be visible. The warmth and sweetness of expression is lost if there is white around the eye.

Ears

The ears should be large and carried drooping. In a fully coated dog the ears actually appear larger than they are, due to the wealth of hair covering them. They should be set slightly below the crown of the skull, contributing to the chrysanthemum-like look.

Mouth

This is wide, slightly undershot or level, and the lips level. An undershot bite is when the outer surface of the upper teeth engages or nearly engages the inner surface of the lower teeth. This is also sometimes called a 'reverse scissor bite'. A level mouth is when the upper and lower teeth meet. The width of the mouth and jaw are important in order to house the correct dentition.

Neck

The neck should be well proportioned, and nicely arched, to carry the head proudly. Again, this will assist with the arrogant look associated with this breed.

Forequarters

The Breed Standard states that the shoulders should be well laid back, referring to the angle of the shoulder blades.

The shoulders should not be excessively heavy, i.e. showing excessive development of muscle, but should flow smoothly from the neck to the shoulder.

The legs should be short and muscular with ample bone, and as straight as possible. The American Breed Standard states that the legs should be straight and that the feet point forward.

The Shih Tzu must not have legs so short that he appears dumpy, or which impede the free movement and stride of the dog, neither should he be too long in leg, throwing him out of all proportion.

Throughout the Breed Standard, there is the reference to proportion. It is essential that all aspects of the dog are in proportion with one another, and that none of these proportions are over exaggerated.

Body

The body is actually slightly longer from between the withers, which is at the root of the neck or highest point of the shoulder, and the root of tail, i.e. from where the tail commences. The depth of the ribcage should extend to just below the elbow; the distance from elbow to wither is a little greater than from elbow to ground. The chest is broad and deep but not overloaded like a barrel. There should be a good spring of rib, not appearing flat or slab-sided (narrow).

Hindquarters

The hindlegs should be short and muscular, with ample bone, straight when viewed from the rear; the thighs are well rounded and muscular. Therefore, the hindquarters will need to be in proportion to the forequarters in order for the correct balance of the dog to be attained.

Feet

The feet are round and well padded; it could be said that they cushion the movement of the dog. They are usually well covered in hair. The American Breed Standard states that dewclaws (equivalent to our thumbs) may be removed.

Tail

In a fully coated dog, the tail is another feature of the Shih Tzu that adds to his glory. The heavily-plumed tail is required to be carried gaily over the back, set on high – in fact, carried at a height approximately level with that of the skull to give a balanced outline. In a really good example, it should be difficult to tell which end is which! A tail carried flat on the dog's back, curly, or set low, will totally detract from the overall balance and outline of the dog.

Gait/movement

Gait is another word for stride or movement. All the above constructional attributes are required in order that the Shih Tzu can be smooth flowing in movement. He should move with ease, floating along proudly and elegantly, alongside his handler. A Shih Tzu needs to be able to reach well forward from the front, and have the same strong power from the rear action.

He is required to show the full black pads from the hind feet as he moves away.

This movement is truly a glorious sight to see in a well-constructed Shih Tzu – like a ship in full sail. However, should any part of the anatomy be incorrect, out of proportion or balance then – like a finely tuned engine of a car – something is likely to break down.

Coat

For a show dog, a full coat is required. The outer coat is long, dense, and not curly, with moderate undercoat which is not woolly. A slight wave to the coat is permitted.

The hair should not affect the dog's ability to see, and length of coat should not restrict movement.

The American Breed Standard is more extravagant, asking for the coat to be luxurious, double coated, dense, long, and flowing. Trimming is listed in the AKC Standard, i.e. feet, bottom of the coat, and around the anus for neatness, but no trimming is mentioned in the English Standard.

Colors

There is a wonderful variety of colors in this breed. The parti colors come in various shades of gold and white, red and white, black and white and grey and white. A white blaze on the forehead and a white tip to the end of the tail is highly prized; it has been said that the Chinese eunuchs in the temples considered these to be lucky dogs. You can get brindle, or brindle and white, or solid colors, such as gold or black, where the dog's coat is one color all over.

Size

The weight in the Breed Standard gives quite a wide scope to this sturdy, little dog i.e. 4.5-8kg (10-18lb), with an ideal weight 4.5-7.5kg (10-16lb), but is counteracted by a height of not more than 27cm (10 ½ inches). I would point out here, that this measurement is from the withers, and not the top of the head. This section also reminds us that type and breed characteristics are of the utmost importance.

The American Breed Standard request that the Shih Tzu's ideal height at withers 9-10 ½in (23-27cm) not less than 8 inches (20.5cm), no more than 11 inches (28cm), with a weight of 9-10lb (4-4.5kg. It states that the breed must be solid, carrying good weight and substance.

Black and white.

Gold and white.

Brindle and white.

Red and white.

Faults

The Breed Standard has given us guidelines to follow, when judging or breeding the Shih Tzu, and that any deviation from these points is considered to be a fault. If we are to be realistic, it is impossible to find an absolutely perfect specimen of the breed, without any fault. Therefore, the seriousness with which the fault should be regarded has to be in exact proportion to its degree, and its effect upon the health and welfare of the dog.

Summing up

The Shih Tzu is a wonderful breed in so many ways, and is the ideal choice of companion for so many people. It is in the hands of our judges and breeders to make sure that Shih Tzu retain all their qualities, especially their marvellous character, temperament and good health.

The American style of presentation.

What do you want from your Shih Tzu?

The Shih Tzu is a wonderful breed to choose, but you must make sure you know exactly what you want from your dog so your dreams of dog ownership match the reality.

Show dog

If you have ambitions to exhibit your Shih Tzu in the show ring, your requirements will be very different from the average pet owner. The requirement for a healthy dog, of sound temperament, must be paramount, but you will also need to find a puppy that conforms as closely as possible to the stipulations of the Breed Standard. If you have set your heart on a particular color, it may take longer to find a suitable puppy.

Bear in mind that exhibiting a Shih Tzu in the show ring is an entirely different prospect to owning one as a pet. There is so much time, care and attention required to care for a Shih Tzu in full show coat.

Unfortunately, it is not a breed that you can decide to show one minute and then not the next, because like any beauty pageant – and let us face it, that is exactly what dog showing is – your exhibit requires daily beauty therapy and attention.

Companion dog

The adaptable Shih Tzu is a delightful dog for people of all ages; he will be a devoted companion for a couple or a person living on their own, and he will be a fun playmate for families, particularly those with slightly older children who will be more appreciative of his needs.

He is also a good breed to choose for those getting on in years, as his exercise needs are moderate. He will enjoy short outings as long as he also has the opportunity to potter around in a garden.

Watch dog

The Shih Tzu can be quite a vocal breed, particularly when he hears strangers approaching. His distant ancestors were kept as watch dogs in the temples of Tibet, and the Shih Tzu of today is alert to all comings and goings. However, if you want a dog to guard your home, think again. A Shih Tzu is more likely to show a burglar around the house than to see him off!

Below: well-trained, well-socialized Shih Tzu will be happy and confident in all situations.

What does your Shih Tzu want from you?

As well as working out what you want from your Shih Tzu, you need to think what he wants from you, and whether you are able to provide it.

Socialization

Socializing puppies is vital if you want well-adjusted adults. In his lifetime, your Shih Tzu will encounter a wide variety of people, he will encounter a wide range of situations, and he may have to adapt to many different places. You need to prepare him for this by working out a program of socialization from puppyhood through to adulthood.

You want a dog that is happy to meet and greet people of all ages, regardless of whether they are

friends or strangers, who will interact peaceably
with other dogs, and who takes the sights and
sounds of the modern world in his stride. It is only by
exposing your Shih Tzu to all these experiences that
he will learn to react calmly and with confidence.

There are so many places that you can take your
puppy to help with his education in meeting people,
and other dogs. Go to the local park or, perhaps,
tuck your puppy under your and visit a car boot
sale or a fete. A Shih Tzu puppy, like many puppies,
is simply irresistible to the general public and
therefore you will find that people will not be able to
contain themselves, and will just have to stop and
chat to you both, which all helps with the puppy's
socializing.

Training

You may think that a small dog, such as a Shih Tzu,
does not need training – but you would be making
a big mistake. All dogs, regardless of size or breed,
need a level of training so they understand their
place in the family.

There are other benefits associated with training
your dog:

- A well-behaved dog is a joy to take anywhere.

- You will enjoy teaching your dog, and will build a strong bond with him.

- You will make lots of new friends, training and socializing your dog.

- Dogs enjoy sensible discipline.

- Everyone benefits from having a well-disciplined dog: the owner, family, friends, neighbors, and the general community.

Love and understanding

A Shih Tzu thrives on companionship and he will repay you with his own very special brand of loyalty and affection. There is no doubt that you will love your little dog – it is almost impossible not to – but you must go one step further and try to understand him.

Work at reading your Shih Tzu's body language; this is a strong indicator of how he is feeling. For example, the tail of a Shih Tzu can tell you much about his mental and physical condition because it acts like a sign.

If at any time our Shih Tzu is on the move and his tail is down, then he is indicating to you that something is wrong. The most common reason is that he feels insecure, wary, or even nervous of someone or something. As soon as he considers the danger or problem has passed, then up will come that tail like a flag of relief.

The dropped tail carriage can also give you an indication that he is unwell, in pain, or he may even have hurt his tail, but remember this only applies to when he is on the move and not when he is resting.

This is just one example of 'reading' your dog, but it shows how important it is to tune into his feelings so that you can react accordingly and safeguard his health and wellbeing. Note that Shih Tzu have a very low pain threshold and will become noticeably very depressed. If your dog ever becomes unwell, he will require plenty of tender loving care.

Extra considerations

Now you have decided the Shih Tzu is the breed for you, the next step is to narrow the choices available so you know exactly what you are looking for.

Male or female?

In general, the Shih has such a laid-back, relaxed temperament that – besides the obvious – there is not much to separate the male from the female especially in temperament. Although both sexes can be strong willed, there is no great dominance feature with the male, as there can be in other breeds.

Males

The male is a happy, fun loving, little chap and is definitely as affectionate, if not slightly more so, than the female. He will reach puberty at quite a young age and is therefore capable of siring puppies from as young as 8½ months.

Do not be fooled by his young puppy look, just bear in mind what he is capable of, especially if you have an unspayed female.

Neutering a male will resolve these problems and is a sensible option for pet owners. However, this is a matter of choice and should be discussed with your vet. If you do have your dog neutered, be sure to watch his weight carefully as, due to the hormonal changes that will take place, he may gain weight. An overweight dog is an unhealthy dog.

If you are intending to show your dog, a male is probably slightly easier to own in some respects because he does not have the six-monthly hormone change, as the females in season do, and is therefore less likely to loose coat.

Females

The female, like the male, is also full of fun – a sweet-natured companion just as anxious to love and be loved. It is normal for her to come into season for the first time anywhere between 6-12 months, and every six months thereafter. However in some bloodlines, bitches only come into season every 12 months. A season lasts for 21-28 days, and during this time, a female must be kept separate from all male dogs. Great care must be taken if you go out for exercise, and she must be secure and safe in your garden.

If your female Shih Tzu is going to be purely a pet – not exhibited or bred from after her show career – it would be more advantageous for her to be spayed.

The female does not need to have a litter of puppies for the sake of her health or wellbeing. In fact, there are health benefits to spaying as it will eliminate the risk of conditions such as pyometra and mammary cancer.

Below: Breeding a litter is a highly specialized business and is therefore best left to the expert.

Your veterinary surgeon will advise you about spaying, which is usually carried out prior to their first season, or midway between seasons. The female, too, is likely to gain weight after spaying so always bear this in mind.

More than one?

Resist the temptation of buying two puppies from the same litter, or of similar ages, as all your time will be needed to look after one puppy.

Early training is essential if your puppy is to grow up to be a loving and disciplined member of your family – this does not happen overnight. It is far better to take on one puppy which will enable you to adhere to a daily routine of handling, grooming, socializing, feeding, house training, as well as instilling general obedience.

Once you have fallen in love with the breed – and consider that you may like to have more than one Shih Tzu – you will find that your first dog will take great delight in helping you to train the new addition. However, it is extremely difficult to housetrain two puppies at the same time.

The Shih Tzu is a very sociable dog and they adore the company of their own breed. It is possible to run a pair of males or females together, in a disciplined

household, without any problem. Of course, there is always the exception to the rule where pure, natural dominance takes over, and one or the other will need to be neutered.

An older dog will accept a youngster coming in, but careful introduction is required as a youngster can be rather exuberant.

Older or rescued dogs

You may wish to skip the puppy stage and take on an older dog – maybe one that has been retired from breeding, lost his owner, or a rescued dog that needs a new home.

There are Shih Tzu rescue services which can be found through breed clubs. The clubs and their secretaries can be contacted via their websites on the internet, or through the national Kennel Club.

When providing a home for an older dog, especially a rescue, do remember that there may well be some teething problems to start with. The dog may be used to an entirely different lifestyle; he may be poorly socialized or not house trained; he may be nervous of strangers due to lack of companionship.

The more you know about the dog's history, the easier it will be to help him to adjust him to his new life, but always remember that kindness, patience and understanding are essential.

Sourcing a puppy

It is so easy to look at lovely, fluffy puppies and possibly fall for the first one you see. But has the breeder given them a good start in life? The time, care and thought that goes into planning and rearing a litter will have a huge impact on the future well-being of the puppies that are produced.

Essentially, you are looking for a fit, clean, happy, healthy puppy that is typical of the breed and is likely to live to a ripe old age. In order to avoid unnecessary heartache it is best to be patient and find the right puppy for you, from the correct source.

Finding a breeder

A good starting place is your national Kennel Club, which has a vast amount of information for both show and pet owners, easily available via the Internet. The next step would be to go to dog shows where you will be able to see a variety of Shih Tzu. This will give you the opportunity to see the different types and colors that are produced.

Wait until a class has been judged, and then talk to the exhibitors – particularly if you have seen a dog you particularly like the look of. Ask questions about the dog's breeding, and his temperament; this is a valuable way of gaining more information about the breed.

The exhibitors you talk to may or may not know about upcoming litters, but if they are unable to help you can do some more research on your national Kennel Club website. You will find contact details for breed clubs, and their secretaries are usually aware of members who have, or are expecting, a litter.

Bear in mind that reputable breeders usually only breed a litter when they want a new puppy to show, and, therefore, there may be a waiting list.

Wait until the puppies are up on their feet and playing actively with each other before going to see them.

Buyer beware!

In your impatience to find a Shih Tzu
puppy, it is all too easy to fall into the trap
of going to an unsuitable source.

Avoid newspapers advertising a litter, or cards
placed in store windows. At best, these could be
the result of an inexperienced pet owner breeding a
litter, and although they may have done a good job,
there are absolutely no guarantees – particularly
regarding the choice of a sire.

All too often, the neighborhood dog will have been
chosen as a good match, without any research into
bloodlines and health issues. Be especially wary of
advertising on the Internet.

There is a danger that the puppies may have come
from a puppy farm, where litters of all breeds are
produced purely for financial gain, with no thought
as to the health, temperament, or rearing of the
puppies involved.

Questions questions, questions

Telephone the breeder of the puppies and ask as many questions as you need to; a reputable breeder will be only too pleased to provide you with as much information as you require.

You will need to find out the following:

- How many puppies are there in the litter?

- What is the split of males and females?

- What colors are available?

- Where have the puppies been reared?

- What socialization have they received?

- How many of the puppies have already been booked?

You should also check the health status of the parents. Like all breeds, the Shih Tzu has some inherited conditions, and you need to ensure the breeder has made the necessary checks and clearances on the breeding stock that has been used.

The breeder will also have lots of questions for you. These may include the following:

- What is the make up of your family?
- If you have children, how old are they?
- Will someone be at home during the day to look after the puppy?
- Do you have a securely fenced garden?
- Do you have plans to show your puppy?

Do not be offended by the barrage of questions. The breeder is only making sure that you can provide a suitable home for one of their precious puppies.

The breeder needs to be sure that you can provide a home for life.

Puppy watching

No sensible breeder should allow anyone to visit puppies when they are first born as this is highly unfair on the nursing mother. She may be adapting to her new family and find strangers an intrusion.

Understandably, visitors want to touch or handle puppies, which in the early stages of a puppy's life can be a little distressing for the mother and risks infection. In the interests of all, it is best to visit puppies when they are on their feet and starting to play and run around, which is generally at five to six weeks of age.

What to look for

The puppies should be reared in the house and be living in clean and comfortable surroundings. Puppies obviously do make a mess and are not house trained at this stage of their life, but there should be no excessive odor from them or the environment in which they are kept.

They should have clean coats and bright eyes, with no discharge, and their rear ends should also be clean and free from any signs of matting or diarrhoea. Their nostrils should be clear and not pinched, causing any difficulty in breathing. You also need to check that there are no umbilical or groin hernias, which are sometimes seen in Shih Tzu, and would require surgery.

The puppies should be brought up in an environment that allows them to become accustomed to household noises, such as voices, television, radio, a vacuum cleaner and a washing machines. This is all part of their socializing to prepare them for the outside world. It is imperative that this takes place at an early stage of their life, as this is when their characters are developing.

The pups should also be well handled by the breeder and family to prepare them for what is to come. If this early regime of socializing is not followed, it can result in nervous puppies that cannot cope with loud noises and with strangers, and this nervousness can stay with them forever.

The mother of the puppies should be available to be seen although, depending on the age of the puppies, she may not be required to be with them constantly once they have started to eat solid food. The dam should also be in a clean and healthy condition, friendly and happy to greet you.

It is not uncommon for the father or sire of the puppies not to be owned by the breeder, as breeders do not keep several male stud dogs at one time. However, the breeder will advise you what recognition he may have in the show ring, making him worthy of being used at stud.

When you visit the puppies they should be full of life, running around playing with each other, responding immediately to your arrival. There should be no sign of nervousness or holding back – there is usually a rush to see which of the littermates reaches you first!

Picking a show puppy

If you are aiming to find a puppy with show potential, it is a good idea to take an experienced person with you who understands the finer points of the Breed Standard.

Shih Tzu puppies are starting to shape up nicely around six weeks, but the best time to choose a show puppy is as near to eight weeks as possible, because what you see at eight weeks is the construction, outline and balance of what that puppy is going to look like as an adult.

All puppies go through growing stages and can change considerably during that time, but if you are patient, then generally what they were at eight weeks, they will be as an adult.

It is so easy to be carried away by how cute the puppies are when you first see them.

All dogs have faults – no dog is perfect – but, for example, the Shih Tzu puppy who shows white around the eyes, has small eyes, or is too short or too long in the leg, whose tail is carried too low, etc, is already at a disadvantage when entering the show ring. However, none of these faults affect the puppy's health or prevent him in any way becoming the most super pet and companion.

A Shih Tzu friendly home

While you are waiting for your new puppy, there are a number of important preparations to make to get your home – and your family – ready for the new arrival. Your house and garden need to be puppy-proofed, you need to buy some basic equipment and, most importantly, you need to draw up some house rules.

These preparations apply to a new puppy but, in reality they are the means of creating an environment that is safe and secure for your Shih Tzu throughout his life.

In the home

Once arriving home with your puppy, you will need to be vigilant as a pup – and, indeed, an adult – can get into all sorts of trouble, usually through no fault of their own.

Security is one of the most important factors; some thought must be given when opening doors, or leaving gates open, as an inquisitive puppy will soon squeeze through in search of adventure.

Take care that the puppy does not go under obstacles that may collapse on him or is allowed to climb on furniture, or up steps or walls, where he can so easily jump off or fall and seriously damage himself.

If there are parts of your house that are out of bounds to the new arrival, then this must be made clear from the onset. Should you decide that your puppy is not allowed upstairs, or not beyond a particular door, a baby gate will assist in keeping this rule.

When using any type of barrier, be sure that it is puppy proof and that your pup cannot squeeze through, resulting in him becoming stuck fast and damaging himself.

Although a puppy will run, play and fall asleep almost anywhere, it is important that he has his own territory to which he can retreat. This personal space represents a place that he knows he can go and feel safe, warm and secure, and where he can rest without any interference from the family (see indoor crates, page 79).

Whatever house rules you have decided upon, you must keep to them, otherwise you are going to have a very confused puppy. For example, if you do not want your pet to sleep upstairs, then he should never be allowed upstairs. It is very unfair and confusing for a puppy if you make one rule one minute, and then break it the next.

In the garden

The Shih Tzu is a very lively and inquisitive little person who has little sense of fear or danger – especially when he has the opportunity to investigate a whole new garden.

If you are an ardent gardener, there may be areas where you do not want your dog to roam. If this is the case, the area should be fenced off so it not a temptation.

The most important consideration is that your garden is 100 per cent safe and secure – it is amazing where a small puppy can manoeuvre himself. Check the gates and the fencing, and do not leave your puppy in the garden unsupervised.

If you have a swimming pool or a pond, extreme care must be taken. Ideally, the area should be fenced off as a totally no go zone for your new addition.

Watching a Shih Tzu puppy scampering and then rolling over on the lawn, will provide you with hours of amusement. A puppy likes nothing more than to end this energetic activity by either lying flat on his back, or with his tummy pressed against the cool grass –front legs reaching forwards and hind legs stretched out behind them. This may not look very comfortable, but it is a typical Shih Tzu trait.

Buying equipment

Shopping for your Shih Tzu is fun – but before
you get carried away, remember there are a few
essential items you will need. If you make good
choices at this stage, the equipment you buy will
last your Shih Tzu for many years – sometimes for
a lifetime.

Indoor crate

This is an invaluable investment, providing your
puppy with his own personal space – and you with
peace of mind.

Make sure you buy a crate that is big enough for your dog to use when he is fully grown. If the door is left open, many adult Shih Tzu prefer it to a dog bed.

When introducing a crate, you want the puppy to associate it with being a safe and happy place to return to and sleep in. Never use the crate as a place of punishment. It should be used when your puppy needs to rest, at times when you cannot supervise him, and to keep him safe overnight. It can also be useful when you are traveling, or staying away in a hotel, or as a safe place to put your youngster if you have visitor that has an allergy, or simply does not like dogs!

Dog beds

What a choice! In this modern day we are presented with a vast array of beds for our pets. There are dog beds ranging from the typical round or oval plastic type, fur lined beds, duvets, igloos and even those that look like proper chairs or couches, in miniature! The Shih Tzu definitely enjoys being pampered and therefore no luxury will go amiss. However, do not be disappointed if you purchase one of the above beds, only to find that your new pet climbs out of it and stretches out full length on the mat or carpet next to it!

It is not essential to spend a great deal of money on purchasing a dog bed, but try to choose one that can be easily washed. Also bear in mind that puppies chew for amusement and when they are cutting their adult teeth, so soft fabrics may be chewed, as well as any toys you put in to occupy your puppy.

Bowls

The Shih Tzu clearly prefers a feeding bowl that is not too deep, which probably stems from the fact that they are a relatively short-nosed breed, and therefore dislike having to lower their heads into a bowl that then becomes too close to their eyes. Purchase a bowl that is not going to tip over easily, and that the puppy can stand close too without loosing his balance.

Stainless steel bowls are easy to clean and wear well, as do the tough, plastic variety now on the market. You must provide fresh drinking water for your puppy. Non-spill bowls are now available from all leading pet stores.

Bear in mind that with a Shih Tzu, the larger the diameter of the top of the water bowl, the wetter his face and moustache are likely to be.

Collar and lead

Iit is essential that your puppy's collar and lead are secure when he goes out and about. I am always amazed at how many owners I see walking their canine companions with collars far too loose. One tug backwards would allow the collar to slip easily over the puppy's head, which could have disastrous consequences.

Naturally the puppy is going to grow and you will need to make sure that the collar is comfortable at all times, neither too tight nor too loose. You should be able to place one finger between the collar and the puppy's neck. A good, lightweight leather or nylon collar and lead, which can be adjusted, will suffice until your Shih Tzu is fully grown – and then you can be tempted by the glorious colors and designs on the market.

ID

Your Shih Tzu must have some form of identity when he goes out in public places. Ideally, he should have an engraved disc attached to his collar with your contact details, and he should also a permanent form of ID, such as a tattoo or a microchip.

Grooming equipment

Daily grooming for a Shih Tzu is essential whether a pet or show puppy. For a pet puppy the basic grooming kit should contain the following:

- Cotton wool pads to wipe around the eyes and face

- A good quality pin brush (no bobbles on the pins)

- A comb with a combination of close-set and wide-set teeth

- A small, soft slicker brush – please note that you would never use this brush on a puppy or dog that is likely to be shown

- Guillotine nail clippers

- Shampoo /conditioner – only use those-made specifically for dogs, as others are likely to dry the coat out too much and can cause irritation.

For more information on grooming, see page 114.

Toys

What fun! Shih Tzu of all ages just love toys and it is such a charming sight to watch them playing. Soft toys are most certainly a favorite and some enjoy the ones that squeak or even play tunes. However, I suspect that most of the toys have been designed to amuse not only the puppy but to entertain the owner as well. You will also find that your Shih Tzu is quite happy to play with the inexpensive, homemade items such as the cardboard centre of a toilet roll, or old woollen socks made safely into a ball.

Extremely hard toys are not usually enjoyed by Shih Tzu and are definitely not recommended for a potential show puppy as they are likely to damage the teeth/bite.

Settling in

At long last, the time has come to collect your Shih Tzu puppy. Try to arrange to collect your puppy in the morning so he has the remainder of the day to settle into his new home. Leaving home can be a traumatic time for a puppy so you want to make this transition as calm and stress free as you can.

Arriving home

When you first arrive home, allow plenty of time to introduce your puppy to his new surroundings. Hopefully, you have insured that everything you need for your new family member is already in place, so you will be able to give him your undivided attention.

The household rules that you have previously decided on will immediately come into use, as probably the first thing your puppy will need is to relieve himself. If you have decided that there is a certain area in your garden to be used for this function, then this should be the puppy's first port of call.

Allow the puppy to explore his new home at his own pace, giving words of reassurance and encouragement where necessary. Even in the short amount of time from collecting your puppy to arriving home, the bond between you and your new arrival will already have started to form.

Meeting the family

Try to avoid too much excitement when introducing the puppy to family members. By far the best and easiest method of introducing a puppy to children is to ask the children to sit quietly on the floor. A lively puppy can so easily wriggle or jump out of your arms, so to avoid any misfortunes; sitting on the floor at the puppy's level is a sensible idea.

It is important to note that when picking up your Shih Tzu you must hold him securely, supporting the front legs and chest with one hand and his hind legs and rear end with the other hand. Most important with this breed, always place the hind legs on the ground first when putting your dog back down, followed gently by his front legs. This prevents your Shih Tzu jumping forwards and landing painfully on his chin.

Facing Page:
Always supervise interactions with young children.

A Shih Tzu, whether a puppy or an adult, can easily break his jaw by falling and landing on his chin, as this is where the impact of the fall will occur.

Meeting the animal family

More introductions may be necessary if you have other pets in the household. A puppy generally can be somewhat pushy, so supervising the first few meetings with another pet is advisable.

If you are introducing your puppy to an established canine resident, then it is best that this takes place outside the house, on neutral territory. Do not allow the puppy to take over the established dog's bed or toys, and make sure that the puppy is not the only canine receiving attention and praise.

Supervise feeding times, making sure that each animal is eating the correct food. If necessary, divide them by a safely closed door, or feed the puppy inside his crate. It is also strongly recommended not to leave a new puppy alone with an older animal until you are absolutely sure all is well. No matter how good a temperament the older animal may have, a young puppy can be somewhat irritating.

A cat and a dog living in the same household can also become good friends, and may even end up sleeping together in the same bed. However, there is always the exception. When introducing a puppy or adult dog to a cat, it is advisable to do this indoors. The gives the cat the opportunity to retreat – by jumping on to something higher – without actually running away. This indoor method of introduction will help you to monitor what is taking place and put a stop to the dog chases cat situation.

A cat will hiss at first and even swipe out with her paws/ claws when first meeting the new canine arrival; this is a cat's normal defence mechanism. This natural, quick reaction by a cat can, of course, cause considerable damage to a puppy's face or eye so make sure initial interactions are supervised.

Feeding

If you purchase your puppy from a reputable breeder, they will provide you with a diet sheet giving you all the feeding instructions you need for your puppy from the time you collect him, when he will be on three or four meals a day, until he becomes a fully grown adult. The diet sheet will also advise you of the puppy's feeding timetable and give you a guide to the quantity of food fed per meal. For more information on diet, see page 102.

Below: *Take care if you keep small animals as pets.*

The first night

Your puppy is going to find the first night away from his littermates very different – it will be very quiet, and he may well feel lonely. He has already experienced major changes to his normal daily routine, and after all this excitement he is now expected to sleep all night in a strange house, in a different bed, on his own – quite a big task for one so little.

Encourage your puppy to toilet for the last time before retiring to bed, as this is going to be part of his new routine as he slowly matures to an adult. The puppy will need to feel warm and safe and may appreciate some soft toys in his bed to cuddle up to as substitutes for his littermates.

Some people leave a low light on for the puppy at night for the first week, considering that he may like to become accustomed to his new home before being left entirely in the dark. Others have tried a radio as company or a ticking clock. Like people, puppies are all individuals and what works for one, does not necessarily work for another. I am afraid it is a matter of trial and error.

If your puppy is sleeping in the kitchen, after making sure that his bed is comfortable, put down some newspaper some slight distance from his bed, which the puppy can use for toileting during the night. Dogs do not normally soil their beds – this only happens when they have been shut in for too long in a confined space.

Be very positive when you leave your puppy on his own; do not linger or keep returning. This will make the situation more difficult. Try very hard not to return at every whimper or you pup will not learn to settle.

Keep to a routine when putting your puppy to bed, so that he knows what is happening and what is expected of him, which in the long run makes him feel secure.

Below: *It is inevitable that your puppy will miss his littermates for the first few nights.*

House training

Like a human baby, a young puppy does not have a lot of control over his bladder and bowels. It can take a Shih Tzu puppy six to eight months before he is reliably house trained. It is not advisable to let the puppy have the run of the house until you have house training under control.

A puppy will want to relieve himself at the following times:

- First thing in the morning

- After mealtimes

- After playing

- On walking up after a nap

- Last thing at night.

A puppy will need to relieve himself at least every two hours; if you give him the opportunity at hourly intervals, this will minimize the risk of accidents. Sometimes it is difficult to recognise when a young puppy squats as they are already so low to the ground, but you will soon spot the tell tale signs of sniffing, turning in circles, running quickly to a specific area and starting to squat. If you wish your puppy to perform outdoors, then as soon as he wakes you must go outside with him to a designated toileting area.

Most owners start off with paper training, which entails placing newspaper close to the back door. As soon as the puppy shows signs of wanting to relieve himself, put the puppy on the newspaper and stay with him, praising him lavishly when he obliges. The area covered by newspaper will need to be larger to start off with and can be reduced at a later stage, until such time as it is no longer required.

You may like to train your puppy to perform to a specific word, e.g. "quickly" which can be very useful in training him to relieve himself on command. Do not make the mistake of putting paper all over the house, as this is inviting the puppy to perform anywhere.

Whenever possible, keep the back door open so that the puppy can go outside to perform. If this is not possible, watch your puppy and as soon as he goes to the newspaper, open the back door and take him out. Stay with the puppy, praising him as he performs.

Some owners use newspaper training throughout a Shih Tzu's life, as it can make life easier when it is pouring with rain or even snowing. To be able to put newspaper down – perhaps on the garage floor – and ask your dog to perform on command can be most helpful. While you are house training your puppy, pick up any rugs or mats as these always seem like an invitation to a youngster.

If you wish your puppy to perform outside, no matter the weather, you must be patient. Do not put the puppy outside expecting him to perform alone. You must go out with him and stay to encourage him. After a short amount of time, and with your encouragement, you will find that as soon as you put the puppy down outside, he will dash off to his usual place and be happy to oblige.

When accidents happen

If you are vigilant, accidents will be kept to a minimum, but should your puppy make a mistake, do not reprimand him, particularly if you discover the accident later. Your puppy will not understand why you are angry with him.

If you catch him in the act, pick him up immediately and put him straight on the newspaper or take him outside, praising him as he performs. If you wish to indicate displeasure to your puppy, the sound of your voice in a gruff "No" is quite sufficient.

If your puppy has had an accident in the house, you must clean the area thoroughly (there are many cleaning solutions from pet stores you can use) otherwise the odor is likely to make the puppy keep returning to the same spot.

Below: Vigilance is the key to successful house training.

Choosing
a diet

The correct food plays such an important part in life, especially for a growing puppy. It is essential that your puppy receives a properly balanced diet if he is going to grow up into a happy, healthy adult, and remain healthy – not only while he is growing, but also throughout his life.

The glory of modern day feeding is that the complete foods have been specially formulated to contain all the natural vitamins and minerals your dog requires. There is no need to add extras of any kind to these foods – in fact, by doing so you can do more harm than good.

Puppy feeding

It is very important that you and your family keep the puppy on the diet that has been recommended by his breeder and, more importantly, that the puppy's digestive system is accustomed to. If an immediate change of diet takes place, it is likely to cause the puppy a digestive upset, possibly resulting in diarrhoea.

A puppy is very clever and will let you know when he no longer requires one of his meals by leaving it untouched. Many useful details should be on the paperwork given to you when you collected the puppy, but if you do have any queries regarding feeding, or in fact anything at all to do with the puppy's welfare, do not hesitate to contact the breeder who will normally be happy to help.

If you do decide to change the puppy's diet for any reason, always do it very gradually. Do not give different types of food on the same day because you will not be able to tell which food agrees with your puppy and which does not.

You will know from the puppy's reaction – and more particularly by the condition of the feces that he passes – whether his digestive system has coped with a new diet or not.

Do not allow your puppy to become a faddy feeder by giving him extra treats with his meal to tempt his appetite.

The clever Shih Tzu will soon get wise to this, and will refuse to eat his food until you have added something he considers particularly appetizing.

Bones and chews

I don't believe you should give a Shih Tzu raw or cooked bone. I have worked with a vet for over 30 years and have seen the sad consequences. Also avoid rawhide bones or chews as these become soft and may lodge in the dog's throat.

Below: Make sure your puppy does not hold out on you for extra treats.

There are plenty of types of artificial bones and chews on the market that safe for your dog, such as the Nylabone range and those that assist in cleaning canine teeth.

If you do feel the need to give your dog something to chew on, then a good, hard, dog biscuit, which is going to break up into smaller pieces and therefore be easily consumed, is a far better option for a Shih Tzu.

If you intend to show your Shih Tzu, you will not be able to give him any hard item that he can chew for fear of causing damage to his face furnishings. The moustache and face furnishings of a Shih Tzu take a very long time to grow, and a considerable amount of time and effort by the owner to keep clean ready for showing – but all can be lost in a matter of minutes!

Feeding regime

To begin with your puppy will need four meals per day, which will all be laid down in the diet sheet given to you by the breeder. To give you a rough idea, the meals are usually given about 8.00 am, 12.00 pm, 4.00 pm and 8.00 pm but, of course, you may have to adjust this slightly to suit your own household.

The diet you feed depends on your Shih Tzu's age and lifestyle.

It will not take too long before the puppy only requires three meals – usually around 10-12 weeks – and eventually by 6-8 months only two meals a day will be necessary.

Naturally, you will need to adjust the size of the meals as the puppy grows; feeding instructions can be provided by the breeder or by the manufacturers of the dog food. Adult Shih Tzu, from 12-18 months, only really require one meal per day but, personally, I have always preferred to split this into two, i.e. breakfast and tea, which has always been appreciated by my canine companions.

When you are aware of the meals required by your new puppy, try to keep mealtimes to a routine: feed at more or less the same times daily, in the same place, and avoid distractions while the puppy is feeding. If you have more than one dog be sure to separate them at mealtimes, feeding the same dog in the same place each time.

Do not to feed your puppy or adult dog immediately before or after vigorous playing or exercise, as this can cause gas to build up in the stomach producing extreme pain and discomfort, bloating of the stomach and even necessitating surgery.

Ideal weight

In order to keep your Shih Tzu in good health it is necessary to monitor his weight. Puppy and adult alike should be neither too thin nor too fat.

The Shih Tzu, although robust should not be allowed to become overweight, as carrying excess weight can cause numerous health problems, affecting the joints, the heart, and other vital organs.

By nature, the Shih Tzu is not a greedy dog, but too many treats can alter this situation. You should not be able to feel a Shih Tzu's ribs easily, but there should be a very slight indication of a waist behind the last rib. Take care not to confuse your dog's weight with the amount of coat he has. Your Shih Tzu should be muscled, and you should not be able to feel soft, excessive fat. Pay extra attention to the male or female Shih Tzu that has been neutered, as they are inclined to gain weight due to the hormone changes that take place, and once this weight has been gained, it is very difficult to lose.

Conversely, a Shih Tzu that is too thin is likely to be an unhealthy dog. It is a sad sight to see a dog's ribs or pin bones protruding, and if you notice a drop in your dog's weight, it could be an indication of health problems. Make sure that you are feeding the correct amount of food for the active or less active dog, and that the dog has a regular worming regime in place.

If you wish to keep an eye on your dog's weight and are unable to do this at home, ask your vet if you can make use of the weighing scales at the practice. You will generally be allowed to do this free of charge, and without an appointment.

Below: It is easier to judge a Shih Tzu's weight when his coat is trimmed.

Caring for your Shih Tzu

The Shih Tzu is quite a robust dog, and does not make excessive demands on his owner. But the coat is a major consideration, particularly if you want to keep your dog in full coat.

If you can ask the breeder to give you a demonstration of how to groom your new puppy this would be most helpful, or perhaps you may have attended a few dog shows when first studying the breed which will have enabled you to pick up some grooming tips. You will learn a tremendous amount by watching someone else groom a Shih Tzu.

Once properly trained, the Shih Tzu loves being groomed and bathed as, if done correctly, he will consider it to be a form of affection and pampering. You will need to groom and attend to your puppy every day, as the Shih Tzu's coat grows quite quickly.

The secret of grooming is to start this program from the day that you collect your puppy. This way, the puppy will learn to accept being groomed, and the coat will not get out of control.

Coat care

You can teach your Shih Tzu to lie on his side on the table in order that you can groom through the different layers of his coat. Make sure that you have hold of him at all times while he is on the table.

At the beginning, you will find this table training a little difficult, but you would be amazed how fast he will learn. Even when he is an adult never take the chance of having him on the table unless he is properly attended.

If at any time during the grooming your Shih Tzu becomes agitated, then just stop for a moment, speak calmly but firmly, and begin again. Never finish until you are both calm!

It is important when brushing the coat to do this properly and not just brush the top coat. Be careful not to be too heavy handed either – scratching the skin with the pins of the brush or pulling at the coat and, hence, the skin. Tease out any small mats or tangles between your fingers, then brush through again.

To make sure that you have done the job properly,

Accustom your puppy to being groomed from an early age.

Most adult Shih Tzu love the special attention they get when they are being groomed.

If your Shih Tzu lies on his side, you will be able to get to all the awkward places.

Once the coat is brushed, you will need to go over it with a wide-toothed comb.

it is always best to check through the coat with the wide-toothed comb.

Allow your puppy to accept the brush around his head, taking great care not to damage his eyes, and then go over the entire head with the wide-toothed comb. Now change to the narrow-toothed comb, and comb his whiskers away from his eyes.

The top-knot

As the hair of a Shih Tzu grows particularly fast across the nose and around the eyes, it is essential to keep this hair out of the eyes to avoid any irritation or damage being caused. In an eight-week-old puppy it is still possible to comb the hair away from the eyes, hence the importance of teaching your youngster how to be handled and groomed.

By five months of age the Shih Tzu is usually ready for his first topknot, which is when the hair on the top of the head has reached sufficient length that it can be put in a special rubber band, to keep the hair out of the dog's eyes.

When putting up the topknot, the hair should be taken from the outer corner of each eye into a reverse V shape at the top of the head.

Facing Page:
The finishing touch:
Tying the topknot.

Coat change

If you have managed to keep a full coat on your puppy until he is about eight months old, then you are doing a really good job. However, from about 8-12 months the Shih Tzu starts to change his coat from a puppy coat to an adult coat, and this is when owners always have the most amount of trouble in grooming, as the baby undercoat matts so easily at this time.

Some puppies lose their puppy coats all over at the same time, whereas others appear to lose the coat in individual areas and at different speeds. No matter how much attention is given to coat care at this time, that puppy coat will change – and this is when the majority of potential new exhibitors and pet owners give in and resort to having the entire coat clipped.

Clipping/trimming

Many new Shih Tzu pet owners start off with the intention of keeping their new edition in full coat, but as the weeks go by and the coat grows, it becomes apparent that, for a pet household, this is sometimes just not going to be possible.

There are other owners who never dreamed of trying to cope with a dog with so much coat, and they have already made up their minds – even before owning the dog – that they would have him clipped.

The age at which a Shih Tzu loses his puppy coat will vary.

When looking for a professional dog groomer, go by recommendation. Look for someone who is accustomed to small dogs and, even better, has actual experience of Shih Tzu. Anyone can pay to take a clipping/trimming course, but this does not mean that they are good at what they do. Going to the grooming parlour can be very frightening for some dogs, so make sure you the groomer is kind and caring. Once your dog has been clipped, he will need to attend the parlour every two or three months.

To keep a pet Shih Tzu in a short trimmed or scissored coat, about 8cm (2-3in) long, as opposed to being clipped down, can be quite difficult. At this length the coat seems to matt easily, especially on the legs and under the armpits.

One of the most popular clipped styles is similar to a puppy look, but where the body and legs are cut down quite short, and the head is either clipped or trimmed, creating a very rounded look. The ears are trimmed to blend in with the shortened beard, and the hair remains on the tail either natural or, has been trimmed down slightly to balance the look of the dog.

Always remember that the hair close to the eyes, in particular, will grow back quite quickly. As the cut hair grows, it is inclined to be rather harsh and spiky and can easily cause irritation to the eyes.

Therefore, more often than not, it requires further attention between full clips.

Bathing the pet Shih Tzu

The Shih Tzu can be bathed as often as you think necessary. It is much better to bath your dog very regularly and not just leave bathing until the dog goes to the grooming parlour. A clean puppy or adult is far easier to groom than a dirty dog and will be much more pleasant to have around your house. You can start bathing from six to eight weeks of age. The first few baths may be a little awkward, but once you have mastered the technique, all will be well.

The show dog

Correct show presentation is quite an art. A show dog needs to be bathed at least once a week and to be kept spotlessly clean and in excellent condition at all times. The head and face furnishings will require daily attention.

One of the best ways to learn about this skill is to ask your breeder or an experienced Shih Tzu exhibitor to demonstrate the entire procedure from beginning to end. By watching an expert, you will be able to see exactly the correct grooming equipment to use for a show dog, how the dog is bathed, conditioned and finally blow-dried.

Below: *It takes a huge amount of hard work to prepare a Shih Tzu for the show ring.*

Once the bathing and blow drying has been carefully completed – bearing in mind this can take from one hour to three hours for an adult Shih Tzu in full coat – the dog must be kept in this condition, in preparation for the show the following day.

The major part of preparing a Shih Tzu for the show ring is carried out at home. On arriving at the show, the entire coat will require to be brushed through, making sure that all has remained in order. The maintenance bands from the head furnishings can now carefully be removed, groomed and prepared for the show topknot, which is customary in the breed.

Regular checks

Your Shih Tzu will require a daily check-up, especially around the eyes as, due to all their hair, it is necessary to comb the moustache away from the eyes. You can control the puppy's head by firmly holding the hair under his chin. This will also enable you to wipe any matter away from the eyes, and clean them with warm water and cotton-wool.

Eye ulcers in Shih Tzu can be so easily caused by sharp objects, a hair or hair clippings irritating the eye, resulting in severe pain and even loss of sight. It is far safer to keep the hair over the top of the nose longer and comb it away from the eyes, than to cut it short and then risk the short hair protruding and damaging the eyes.

A general daily groom and check-up will only take about 20 minutes, whereas leaving the coat to turn into a matted mess will not only be difficult and time consuming to put right, but also very unpleasant for all concerned. It is always best to make sure, on a daily basis, that both ends of a Shih Tzu are clean. You will find it less difficult to hose down and shampoo the rear end of a Shih Tzu and then dry it, than to try and clean them up in a half-hearted fashion. Wet wipes, a towel and talcum powder can help, until you are able to do the job properly.

You may need help with cutting nails.

Hair growing between the pads should to be trimmed.

You may need to pluck hairs from inside the ears.

Teeth need cleaning on a regular basis.

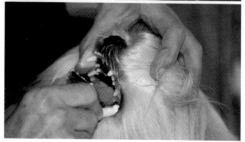

Ears and nails

Not many Shih Tzu pet owners, quite rightly, feel confident enough to cut their dogs nails, or remove the hair from the inside of the dog's ears. Neither of these tasks should be attempted unless prior professional instruction has been given, as it is possible to do more harm than good. Seek advice from your puppy's breeder, an experienced Shih Tzu owner, or you can book an appointment with your vet who will do the job form you.

Teeth

The teeth of a Shih Tzu are quite small and not very strong; therefore playing with toys that pull or tug is not recommended, regardless of the dog's age. A puppy is very slow to cut his teeth and can go through very uncomfortable times, with sore gums, and may breathe through his mouth instead of his nose.

Keep a check on your puppy's teeth now and throughout his life. You can train your puppy from about 10 months to have his teeth cleaned with dog toothpaste (do not use the human variety), or if you find this too difficult there are various gels and powders specially made for dogs. Your veterinary surgeon will give advice.

Exercising your Shih Tzu

To avoid any risk of contracting infectious dog diseases, you should not allow your puppy to mix with or walk on ground where other dogs have exercised, until such time as his inoculations have been completed and kicked in. You can start to train your puppy to a collar and lead, in your own back garden, so that when the time comes for him to go for a walk, he will have an idea of what is required.

As an adult this is a breed that is happy to take virtually as much, or as little, exercise that you wish to give him. But to begin with, as a tiny puppy, it is not sensible to walk him very far as, at this early stage, damage can be done to joints and ligaments. A good way of considering a puppy's exercise is to think of a human toddler and how far they are capable or happy to walk before having to be picked up.

The glory of the size of a Shih Tzu puppy is that you can walk him a little and then carry him, which enables you to get him out and about, starting to meet the world and socialize. I would stress here that you should only pick up and carry your Shih Tzu until his inoculations are finished, or in emergencies, otherwise this could become a very bad habit.

The older Shih Tzu

Like elderly people, the older your Shih Tzu becomes, the more understanding, care and attention he is likely to need and deserve. He will start to look elderly around the age of 10-12 years; his joints may become stiff and painful with arthritis, probably his hearing will not be as good as it was, and there could be deterioration in his sight. He will be sleeping much more and will be less inclined to take exercise; it may be necessary to change his diet to suit his digestive system.

Do not consider that just because he is elderly that nothing can be done to help him. In fact, just the opposite applies as, at this time in his life, you should have him health checked more frequently. Early detection and prompt medical assistance can add years to an elderly dog's life.

Do, however, allow him to be an old age pensioner, and do not expect him to do all the things he used to do. He is beginning to wind down now, so insisting that he goes for a long walk is likely to do more harm than good. Adjust his lifestyle to suit his slower pace, and try to keep him in some form of routine. A little sensible exercise is good for him, as it helps to keep him from stiffening up, stimulates his mind, increases his appetite (which is probably not as good as it was), and keeps his bowels moving, too!

Letting go

To say a final farewell to your beloved Shih Tzu is an extremely heart rending task and the moment which owners dread.

If we are to lose our pets, if they could just quietly slip away in their sleep it would make matters slightly easier to bear. On some occasions this does happen, but more often, we, as loving, responsible owners, have to make the decision to let them go. The questions nearly every owner asks are: "is this the right time?" and "are we doing the right thing?"

After spending so many wonderful years with your dog, probably from a puppy through to old age, you will know your dog best. You will realize how he was as a youngster and what his capabilities and quality of life are in his final years.

Elderly dogs can become very distressed if they cannot stand or walk properly. Perhaps they are no longer clean in the house, or worse, they are in pain and life is just too much of a struggle. When this time comes and their quality of life has diminished, then it will be time to let go.

Your veterinary surgeon and nursing staff will help to guide you through this sad process, either at the surgery or in your own home. The vet will also be able to assist you with any specific requests and give you details regarding cremation or a pet cemetery for your beloved companion.

All the good times and memories that you shared with your beloved Shih Tzu, will stay with you forever, but taking on a new puppy or a rescued dog may help to lighten your heart. A new addition to the household who will seek your attention, keep you occupied, get you out and about – and put a smile on your face – has to be good news, for you, and your delightful new family member.

Training guidelines

How often have you heard people say: "education is a marvellous thing"? Well, this could not be more true, and the Shih Tzu is a highly intelligent 'little person' who is capable of learning as much as you are prepared to teach him.

Having said that, the Shih Tzu is strong minded and although not actually disobedient, his preference is to do what is required of him, but in his own way and at his own pace.

When you are training, it will help if you try to stick to the following guidelines:

- Keep training sessions short and positive. A puppy, in particular, has a short attention span and his work will deteriorate if you continue for too long.

- Make sure you reward your Shih Tzu frequently, either with treats, or maybe have a game with a favorite toy.

- Do not train after your Shih Tzu has eaten, or when he has just returned from exercise. He will be either too full, or too tired to concentrate.

- Choose a training area that is free from distractions so your Shih Tzu will focus on you.

- Try not to confuse your dog by using long sentences when only a single word is required. Remember, your Shih Tzu – clever though he is – does not speak English, so keep it simple!

- Tone of voice is more important than what you say. If you said: "Sophie, come" in a deep, gruff manner, this tone is unlikely to encourage poor Sophie. If on the other hand you called: "Sophie, come"' in a higher pitched, light-hearted tone, it would be far more inviting, indicating how important the tone of your voice is to your canine companion.

- If other members of your family want to get involved in training, make sure everyone uses the same commands.

- If your Shih Tzu is struggling with an exercise, go back a stage so you can reward him.

- Always end training sessions on a positive note – training should be fun for you and your Shih Tzu.

First lessons

There are a number of basic obedience exercises to teach your Shih Tzu. With a bit of patience – and bribery – it will not take him long to master them.

Wearing a collar

Collar training can begin at home, even before the puppy has finished his inoculations. Put the collar on for about half an hour at a time so that the puppy can become accustomed to wearing this strange object around his neck.

At first he will probably dislike the collar; he may sit still and refuse to move, or scratch at the collar and even walk backwards, in an effort to try and remove it. The best way to deal with all these reactions is to distract his attention with toys, or by playing with him, and all will soon be forgotten.

Allow the puppy to run around and play while wearing his collar and slowly increase the amount of time that he is wearing it, but never leave him unsupervised.

It is not advisable for a Shih Tzu puppy or adult to wear a collar full time when at home, unless the coat is clipped short, as it is liable to become entangled in the coat, causing problems and irritation.

Lead training

Some Shih Tzu puppies take to lead training straightaway, with no problems whatsoever, and off they go without a care in the world. But you may have puppy who simply hates the lead, and when he experiences the slightest tension, he cries, lies down and refuses to budge, rolls on his back or catapults forward in a mad burst of energy. But fear not, help is at hand.

The best way of introducing a Shih Tzu puppy to a lead is in his own home. Attach the lead to the puppy's collar and allow him to move around the garden with the lead trailing behind, making sure it does not get tangled up.

While the lead is attached to the puppy's collar, distract him by fussing, talking and playing with him in a very light-hearted, upbeat manner. After a few lessons, when the puppy has become accustomed to the lead, you will be able to hold the end of the lead. Make sure that at first, you go where the puppy wants to go to avoid any tension on the puppy's neck.

Be sure to praise your puppy for any directional moves, no matter how small they may be. The next step is for you to go to the end of the lead and encourage your puppy towards you.

If the puppy still refuses to move, you may need to get down to the puppy's level to begin with, but as soon as the puppy reaches you, do not forget the praise!

Unless you are planning to get involved in competitive obedience, where dogs are trained to walk on the left, it will not matter which side of you the dog walks, but it will help if you introduce a verbal cue, such as "Heel" or "Close".

Come when called

Calling your dog to come to you on command has to be the most important lesson any dog should learn. You will be relieved to know that the Shih Tzu as an adult, although not the most obligingly obedient little dog, will come to you when called, but probably when he is ready...

You can start training your puppy to "Come" as soon as he arrives in his new home. At eight weeks the puppy will be very responsive to you, and will want to be with you all the time. Sit on the floor, clap your hands a couple of times to attract attention, call the puppy's name followed by "Come" and, hey presto, here he comes!

Now give him plenty of praise, and maybe a treat, so that the puppy knows every time he returns to you, he is praised.

Never scold a puppy or an adult for coming to you – no matter how long he takes – otherwise he will associate being scolded with returning to you, which will not be a great incentive.

Training can progress by adding distance and distractions. Go out into the garden, and try calling your puppy. Make sure you have a really tasty treat to hand, so he learns that it is always rewarding to come when he is called.

If he is slow to respond, make yourself more exciting by using a high-pitched voice, jumping up and down, or maybe running off in the opposite direction. It does not matter how silly you look or sound, you must be irresistible to your puppy. The best form of training is when your dog thinks it is all one big game.

If your trainee is really not paying attention, then you can teach this lesson with the assistance of a long lead which will give the puppy a gentle reminder to return to you.

Do not allow your Shih Tzu free running exercise away from home until you are confident that he has mastered the recall.

Stationary exercises

These exercises are easy to teach and you, and your Shih Tzu, will be inspired by your success!

"Sit"

You may have noticed that your Shih Tzu naturally sits for various reasons, such as when presented with food or a toy. If you capitalise on this, it is an excellent way to begin training.

At every opportunity, give your Shih Tzu the verbal cue, "Sit". Make sure you only use the word "sit" – not "sit down" – as this is combining two different exercises.

To progress your training, you can use a treat, held just above your puppy's head. As he looks up at the treat, he will transfer his weight back on his hindquarters and go into the sit position.

Practice this a few times, and then introduce he verbal cue. Soon your puppy will react to the verbal cue and will not need to be lured into position. However, it is a good idea to reward your Shih Tzu on a random basis to keep him on his toes!

"Down"

The Down position is a natural progression from the Sit. Ask your puppy to "Sit", and, making sure he knows you have a treat in your hand, hold it in front of his nose and lower it towards the ground.

The puppy will follow the treat, often going down on his front legs to begin, followed by his hindquarters as he tries to get the treat. Keep the treat in your hand until your puppy is in the Down position, and then reward him.

Keep practicing, and when your puppy understands what is required, introduce the verbal cue, "Down".   Gradually extend the time he stays in the Down before rewarding him.

"Stand"

Show dogs need to learn to "Stand" on command. In fact, exhibitors often choose this in preference to a Sit, as a show dog is always expected to stand in the show ring.

Training begins from as early as six weeks old when a puppy is 'stacked' which means actually putting him in the standing position. To begin with your puppy will try to wriggle out of position, but use a treat to help him maintain his position for just a few seconds before rewarding him.

Keep practising and when your puppy understands the exercise, introduce the verbal cue, "Stand".

Control exercises

The Shih Tzu is full of fun and has boundless energy when he is enjoying one of his playful periods. This means that he can find it difficult to inhibit his behavior, but it is important to establish control for his own safety as well as earning his respect.

"Stay"

This command is used as an attachment to a position that has already been achieved, such staying in a Sit, a Stand or in the Down position. First put your puppy in the position you require; most dogs are more likely to remain in position in the Down, as this is most comfortable for them.

Now give a firm hand signal, with the palm of your hand towards the puppy, and take two steps to the side.

Alternatively, you can face your puppy, and take two steps back. Return to your pup and praise and reward him before he has a chance to break position. Keep practicing and then introduce the verbal cue, "Stay".

Do not bend down or make direct eye contact with your puppy whilst teaching the Stay position as this will be seen as an invitation to join you. Gradually extend the distance, and the time, you can leave your puppy, making sure you give lots of praise, and a treat, when the exercise is finished.

"Wait"

This is a word to use when you want to postpone or delay an action. Basically it means: "wait until I give you the next instruction". The sound of the word "Wait" should be sharp and very positive to attract the attention of your puppy, placing him on standby until you deliver his next instruction.

The Wait command can be used for many useful purposes, especially in the interests of your dog's safety, such as opening car doors, putting on the lead, or crossing the road. It can also be used when throwing toys for your puppy to retrieve or when putting his dinner down.

As with the Stay, the Wait exercise is taught from the Sit, Stand or Down positions.

You need to differentiate it from the Stay by stepping forward, with your back to the puppy, and then giving a hand signal with your palm pointing towards him. This may seem like a subtle difference, but the clever Shih Tzu will read your body language and, with practice, he will understand what is required.

Below: *Your Shih Tzu must "Wait" until you give the next command.*

"No" or "Leave"

These two words are very useful when training any breed of dog. Apart from the puppy's name, "No" is quite likely to be one of the first words your puppy will learn when you want to stop him misbehaving. It is used most often when you want to stop your puppy in his tracks – often for his own safety.

As previously mentioned, any command that you give to you dog will have far more effect if the correct tone of your voice accompanies the command. The tone of voice you use for "No" should be deep and quite gruff.

The instruction to "Leave" is usually associated with a retrieve situation, such as a toy or a dumb bell. This command can be taught quite easily when first playing with your puppy. As you gently take a toy from his mouth, introduce the verbal cue, "Leave", and then praise him.

If he is reluctant, swap the toy for another toy or a treat, do not get involved in a tug-of-war with the puppy. Not only could this seriously damage a Shih Tzu's mouth and jaw, but also he will become over excited which could, if allowed to continue, cause a change in the puppy's temperament.

Facing Page:
There are times when your puppy needs to respond to the "Leave" command.

The ideal owner

The mistake made by many owners of small dogs is treating the dog like a pampered, spoilt child. This does the dog no favours, and it can lead to major problems as the dog fails to understand his place in the family.

The Shih Tzu is as bright as a button, and he will fall into bad habits as quickly as he will learn good ones. It is your job to start as you mean to go on, establishing a regime of firmness, kindness and consistency. A dog that understands the rules that govern his life will be far more content than one who is subject to the unpredictable behavior of an over-indulgent owner.

The Shih Tzu has the intelligence to learn all that you wish to teach him, but he also has the charm to be able to bring his owner around to his way of thinking! Only the Shih Tzu in question will be able to vote to find out if you are to turn out to be the ideal owner!

Opportunities for Shih Tzu

Although the Shih Tzu loves the comfort and security of his own home, like the majority of us, he also enjoys being out and about, meeting new people and other animals. In order to develop and appreciate this intelligent little dog's full character and potential, you can get involved with some of the canine sports and activities on offer.

Good Citizen Scheme

The Kennel Club Good Citizen Scheme was introduced to promote responsible dog ownership, and to teach dogs basic good manners. In the US there is one test; in the UK there are four award levels: Puppy Foundation, Bronze, Silver and Gold.

Exercises within the scheme include:

- Walking on lead

- Road walking

- Control at door/gate.

- Food manners

- Recall

- Stay

- Send to bed

- Emergency stop.

Showing

The Shih Tzu is one of the most difficult breeds to exhibit in the show ring, which has nothing to do with any problem in the breed whatsoever, but purely because of the coat care and presentation required. Over the years, presentation in the show ring has improved dramatically and therefore to present the Shih Tzu correctly for showing, requires not only time and patience, but also considerable skill. To attain the standard at which these dogs are shown this necessitates experienced daily coat care and is definitely not for the faint hearted, nor anyone who is not prepared to keep to a proper grooming regime.

Competitive obedience

This is a sport where you are assessed as a dog and handler, completing a series of exercises including heelwork, recalls, retrieves, stays, sendaways and scent discrimination.

The Shih Tzu is not a natural Obedience dog, but he is more than capable of learning and performing the exercises. These are relatively simple to begin with, involving heelwork, a recall and stays in the lowest class, and, as you progress, more exercises are added, and the aids you are allowed to give are reduced.

To achieve top honours in this discipline requires intensive training, as precision and accuracy are of paramount importance.

Agility

In this sport, the dog completes an obstacle course under the guidance of his owner. You need a good element of control, as the dog completes the course off the lead.

In competition, each dog completes the course individually and is assessed on both time and accuracy. The dog that completes the course in the fastest time, with the fewest faults, wins the class. The obstacles include an A-frame, a dog-walk, weaving poles, a seesaw, tunnels, and jumps.

There are different size categories, and with lots of patience and positive training, the Shih Tzu can be an able competitor.

Heelwork to music

Also known as Canine Freestyle, this activity is becoming increasingly popular. Dog and handler perform a choreographed routine to music, allowing the dog to show off an array of tricks and moves, which delight the crowd.

The Shih Tzu has the out-going personality for this discipline, but there may be times when he takes the initiative and does a little Shih Tzu improvisation!

|Health care

We are fortunate that the Shih Tzu is a healthy dog and, with good routine care, a well-balanced diet, and sufficient exercise, most will experience few health problems.

However, it is your responsibility to put a program of preventative health care in place – and this should start from the moment your puppy, or older dog, arrives in his new home.

Vaccinations

Dogs are subject to a number of contagious diseases. In the old days, these were killers, and resulted in heartbreak for many owners. Vaccinations have now been developed, and the occurrence of the major infectious diseases is now very rare. However, this will only remain the case if all pet owners follow a strict policy of vaccinating their dogs.

There are vaccinations available for the following diseases:

Adenovirus: (Canine Adenovirus): This affects the liver; affected dogs have a classic 'blue eye'.

Distemper: A viral disease which causes chest and gastro-intestinal damage. The brain may also be affected, leading to fits and paralysis.

Parvovirus: Causes severe gastro enteritis, and most commonly affects puppies.

Leptospirosis: This bacterial disease is carried by rats and affects many mammals, including humans. It causes liver and kidney damage.

Rabies: A virus that affects the nervous system and is invariably fatal. The first signs are abnormal behavior when the infected dog may bite another animal or a person. Paralysis and death follow. Vaccination is compulsory in most countries. In the UK, dogs traveling overseas must be vaccinated.

Kennel Cough: There are several strains of Kennel Cough, but they all result in a harsh, dry, cough. This disease is rarely fatal; in fact most dogs make a good recovery within a matter of weeks and show few signs of ill health while they are affected. However, kennel cough is highly infectious among dogs that live together so, for this reason, most boarding kennels will insist that your dog is protected by the vaccine, which is given as nose drops.

Lyme Disease: This is a bacterial disease transmitted by ticks (see page 170). The first signs are limping, but the heart, kidneys and nervous system can also be affected. The ticks that transmit the disease occur in specific regions, such as the north-east states of the USA, some of the southern states, California and the upper Mississippi region. Lyme disease is still rare in the UK so vaccinations are not routinely offered.

Vaccination program

In the USA, the American Animal Hospital Association advises vaccination for core diseases, which they list as: distemper, adenovirus, parvovirus and rabies. The requirement for vaccinating for non-core diseases – leptospriosis, Lyme disease and kennel cough – should be assessed depending on a dog's individual risk and his likely exposure to the disease.

In the UK, vaccinations are routinely given for distemper, adenovirus, leptospirosis and parvovirus.

In most cases, a puppy will start his vaccinations at around eight weeks of age, with the second part given a fortnight later. However, this does vary depending on the individual policy of veterinary practices, and the incidence of disease in your area.

You should also talk to your vet about whether to give annual booster vaccinations. This depends on an individual dog's levels of immunity, and how long a particular vaccine remains effective.

Parasites

No matter how well you look after your Shih Tzu, you will have to accept that parasites – internal and external – are ever present, and you need to take preventative action.

Internal parasites: As the name suggests, these parasites live inside your dog. Most will find a home in the digestive tract, but there is also a parasite that lives in the heart. If infestation is unchecked, a dog's health will be severely jeopardized, but routine preventative treatment is simple and effective.

External parasites: These parasites live on your dog's body – in his skin and fur, and sometimes in his ears.

Roundworm

This is found in the small intestine, and signs of infestation will be a poor coat, a pot belly, diarrhoea and lethargy. Pregnant mothers should be treated, but it is almost inevitable that parasites will be passed on to the puppies. For this reason, a breeder will start a worming program, which you will need to continue. Ask your vet for advice on treatment, which will need to continue throughout your dog's life.

Tapeworm

Infection occurs when fleas and lice are ingested; the adult worm takes up residence in the small intestine, releasing mobile segments (which contain eggs) which can be seen in a dog's feces as small rice-like grains. The only other obvious sign of infestation is irritation of the anus. Again, routine preventative treatment is required throughout your Shih Tzu's life.

Heartworm

This parasite is transmitted by mosquitoes, so it is more likely to be present in areas with a warm, humid climate. It is found in all parts of the USA, although its prevalence does vary. It is rarely seen in the UK.

Heartworm live in the right side of the heart. Larvae can grow up to 14 ins (35.5cm) in length. A dog with heartworm is at severe risk from heart failure, so preventative treatment, as advised by your vet, is essential. Dogs living in the USA should have regular blood tests to check for the presence of infection.

Lungworm

Lungworm, or *Angiostrongylus vasorum*, is a parasite that lives in the heart and major blood vessels supplying the lungs. It can cause many problems, such as breathing difficulties, excessive bleeding, sickness and diarrhoea, seizures, and can even be fatal. The parasite is carried by slugs and snails, and the dog becomes infected when ingesting these, often accidentally when rummaging through undergrowth.

Lungworm is not common, but it is on the increase Fortunately, it is easily preventable and even affected dogs usually make a full recovery if treated early enough. Your vet will be able to advise you on the risks in your area and what form of treatment may be required.

Fleas

A dog may carry dog fleas, cat fleas, and even human fleas. The flea stays on the dog only long enough to have a blood meal and to breed, but its presence will result in itching and scratching.

If your dog has an allergy to fleas – which is usually a reaction to the flea's saliva – he will scratch himself until he is raw.

Spot-on treatment, which should be administered on a routine basis, is easy to use and highly effective on fleas. You can also treat your dog with a spray or with insecticidal shampoo. Bear in mind that your dog's whole living area will need to be sprayed, and all other pets living in your home will also need to be treated.

How to detect fleas

You may suspect your dog has fleas, but how can you be sure? There are two methods to try.

Run a fine comb through your dog's coat, and see if you can detect the presence of fleas on the skin, or clinging to the comb. Alternatively, sit your dog on some white paper and rub his back. This will dislodge feces from the fleas, which will be visible as small brown specks. To double check, shake the specks on to some damp cotton-wool. Flea feces consists of the dried blood taken from the host, so if the specks turn a lighter shade of red, you know your dog has fleas.

Ticks

These are blood-sucking parasites which are most frequently found in rural area where sheep or deer are present. The main danger is their ability to pass Lyme disease to both dogs and humans. Lyme disease is prevalent in some areas of the USA (see page 165), although it is still rare in the UK. You should discuss the best product to use to control ticks with your vet.

How to remove a tick

If you spot a tick on your dog, do not try to pluck it off as you risk leaving the hard mouth parts embedded in his skin. The best way to remove a tick is to use a fine pair of tweezers or you can buy a tick remover. Grasp the tick head firmly and then pull the tick straight out from the skin. If you are using a tick remover, check the instructions, as some recommend a circular twist when pulling. When you have removed the tick, clean the area with mild soap and water.

Ear mites

The signs of infestation are a brown, waxy discharge, and your dog will continually shake his head and scratch his ear. If you suspect your Shih Tzu has ear mites, a visit to the vet will be need so that medicated ear drops can be prescribed.

Fur mites

These small, white parasites are often referred to as 'walking dandruff'. They cause a scurfy coat and mild itchiness. However, they are zoonetic – transferable to humans – so prompt treatment with an insecticide prescribed by your vet is essential.

Harvest mites

These are picked up from the undergrowth, and can be seen as a bright orange patch on the webbing between the toes, although this can be found elsewhere on the body, such as on the ear flaps. Treatment is effective with the appropriate insecticide.

Skin mites

There are two types of parasite that burrow into a dog's skin. *Demodex canis* is transferred from a mother to her pups while they are feeding. Treatment is with a topical preparation, and sometimes antibiotics are needed.

The other skin mite is *Sarcoptes scabiei*, causes intense itching and hair loss. It is highly contagious, so all dogs in a household will need to be treated, which involves repeated bathing with a medicated shampoo.

Common ailments

As with all living animals, dogs can be affected by a variety of ailments. Most can be treated effectively after consulting with your vet, who will prescribe appropriate medication and will advise you on how to care for your dog's needs.

Here are some of the more common problems that could affect your Shih Tzu, with advice on how to deal with them.

Anal glands

These are two small sacs on either side of the anus, which produce a dark-brown secretion which dogs use when they mark their territory. The anal glands should empty every time a dog defecates but if they become blocked or impacted, a dog will experience increasing discomfort.

A Shih Tzu with impacted anal glands may nibble at his rear end, or 'scoot' his bottom along the ground to relieve the irritation.

Treatment involves a trip to the vet where the vet will empty the glands manually. It is important to do this without delay or infection may occur.

Dental problems

The Shih Tzu can be prone to dental problems so, as highlighted earlier, good dental hygiene will do much to minimize problems with gum infection and tooth decay.

If tartar accumulates to the extent that you cannot remove it by brushing, the vet will need to intervene. In a situation such as this, an anesthetic will need to be administered so the tartar can be removed manually.

Diarrhoea

There are many reasons why a dog has diarrhoea, but most commonly it is the result of scavenging, a sudden change of diet, or an adverse reaction to a particular type of food.

If your dog is suffering from diarrhoea, the first step is to withdraw food for a day. It is important that he does not dehydrate, so make sure that fresh drinking water is available. However, drinking too much can increase the diarrhoea, which may be accompanied with vomiting, so limit how much he drinks at any one time.

After allowing the stomach to rest, feed a bland diet, such as white fish or chicken with boiled rice for a few days. In most cases, your dog's motions will return to normal and you can resume normal feeding, although this should be done gradually.

However, if this fails to work and the diarrhoea persists for more than a few days, you should consult you vet. Your dog may have an infection which needs to be treated with antibiotics, or the diarrhoea may indicate some other problem which needs expert diagnosis.

Ear infections

The Shih Tzu has long feathering on his ears, so air will not circulate as easily as it in dogs with semi-pricked or pricked ears. This means that a Shih Tzu is more prone to ear infections.

A healthy ear is clean with no sign of redness or inflammation, and no evidence of a waxy brown discharge or a foul odor. If you see your dog scratching his ear, shaking his head, or holding one ear at an odd angle, you will need to consult your vet.

The most likely causes are ear mites, an infection, or there may a foreign body, such as a grass seed, trapped in the ear.

Depending on the cause, treatment is with medicated ear drops, possibly containing antibiotics. If a foreign body is suspected, the vet will need to carry our further investigations.

Eye problems

The Shih Tzu has shallow eye sockets and prominent eyes, which means that the eyeballs are more vulnerable than in other breeds. It is not unusual for the eye to be injured by a thorn, or some other sharp object, so take care where you exercise your dog.

If your Shih Tzu's eyes look red and sore, he may be suffering from conjunctivitis. This may, or may not be accompanied with a watery or a crusty discharge. Conjunctivitis can be caused by a bacterial or viral infection, it could be the result of an injury, or it could be an adverse reaction to pollen.

You will need to consult your vet for a correct diagnosis, but in the case of an infection, treatment with medicated eye drops is effective.

Conjunctivitis may also be the first sign of more serious inherited eye problems (see page 186).

In some instances, a dog may suffer from dry, itchy eye, which your dog may further injure through scratching. This condition, known as keratoconjunctivitis sicca, may be inherited.

Foreign bodies

In the home, puppies – and some older dogs – cannot resist chewing anything that looks interesting. The toys you choose for your dog should be suitably robust to withstand damage, but children's toys can be irresistible. Some dogs will chew – and swallow – anything from socks, tights, and any other items from the laundry basket to golf balls and stones from the garden. Obviously, these items are indigestible and could cause an obstruction in your dog's intestine, which is potentially lethal.

The signs to look for are vomiting, and a tucked up posture. The dog will often be restless and will look as though he is in pain.

In this situation, you must get your dog to the vet without delay as surgery will be needed to remove the obstruction.

Heatstroke

The Shih Tzu is one of the brachycephalic dog breeds, which include the Pekingese, the Bulldog, the Pug and the Lhasa Apso. All these dogs have a shorter muzzle than most other breeds, and a flatter nose. Although this feature should not be exaggerated, it does mean that these breeds may have more labored breathing and, as a result, they will overheat more easily.

On hot days, make sure your dog always has access to shady areas, and wait for a cooler part of the day before going for a walk. Be extra careful if you leave your Shih Tzu in the car, as the temperature can rise dramatically even on a cloudy day. Heatstroke can happen very rapidly, and unless you are able lower your dog's temperature, it can be fatal.

If your Shih Tzu appears to be suffering from heatstroke, lie him flat and try to reduce his core body temperature by wrapping him in cool towels. A dog should not be immersed in cold water as this will cause the blood vessels to constrict, impeding heat dissipation. As soon as he made some recovery, take him to the vet, where cold intravenous fluids can be administered.

Lameness/limping

There are a wide variety of reasons why a dog can go lame from a simple muscle strain, to a fracture, ligament damage, or more complex problems with the joints. If you are concerned about your dog, do not delay in seeking help.

As your Shih Tzu becomes more elderly, he may suffer from arthritis, which you will see as general stiffness, particularly when he gets up after resting. It will help if you ensure his bed is in a warm draught-free location, and if your Shih Tzu gets wet after exercise, you must dry him thoroughly.

If you Shih Tzu seems to be in pain, consult your vet who will be able to help with pain relief medication.

Skin problems

If your dog is scratching or nibbling at his skin, first check he is free from fleas (see page 169). There are other external parasites which cause itching and hair loss, but you will need a vet to help you find the culprit.

An allergic reaction is another major cause of skin problems. It can be quite an undertaking to find the cause of the allergy, and you will need to follow your vet's advice, which often requires eliminating specific ingredients from the diet, as well as looking at environmental factors.

Inherited disorders

There are a number of conditions that can be passed on from one generation to the next, and there are some disorders that a particular breed will be more likely to inherit. Although breeders strive to eliminate these problems from their bloodlines, it is important to research thoroughly before buying a puppy.

Eye conditions

The Shih Tzu is predisposed to a number of inherited eye conditions, and some are due to the structure of his skull. As highlighted earlier, brachycephallic breeds have a foreshortened muzzle; they also have shallow eye sockets which makes the eyes more prominent. In some dogs, this can result in an inability to close both eyelids over the eye. This can

cause a condition known as exposure keratitis which causes inflammation and ulceration of the cornea.

The Shih Tzu can also suffer from proptosis, where the eyelids clamp shut behind the eyeball, cutting off the blood supply to the retina. This is a real emergency and urgent veterinary help must be sought in order to save the eye.

Other inherited eye conditions include the following:

Hereditary Cataracts: These may affect one or both eyes. The clouding of the lens may be complete or partial, which will determine how much vision remains. The Canine Eye Registration Foundation (CERF), in the US, recommends annual eye testing.

Entropion: This is an in-turning of the eyelids, which means that the eyeball is often irritated by in-growing eyelashes. Surgical correction is generally successful.

Distichiasis: A double row of eyelashes is present, and one or both may rub on the surface of the cornea. Surgical removal of the eyelashes is usually required.

Keratoconjunctivitis sicca: This condition, also known as dry eye, is when there is inadequate tear production. The eye becomes dry and itchy; the cornea may become ulcerated or scarred, resulting in loss of vision. Treatment is geared to stimulating the tear glands, and administering artificial 'tears' for the rest of the dog's life.

Progressive Retinal Atrophy: This is a degeneration of the eye nerves, which starts as night blindness and deteriorates to blindness. There is no treatment.

Summing up

It may give the pet owner cause for concern to find about health problems that may affect their dog. But it is important to bear in mind that acquiring some basic knowledge is an asset, as it will allow you to spot signs of trouble at an early stage. Early diagnosis is very often the means to the most effective treatment.

Fortunately, the Shih Tzu is a generally healthy and disease-free dog with his only visits to the vet being annual check-ups. In most cases, owners can look forward to enjoying many happy years with this affectionate and highly entertaining companion.

Useful addresses

Breed & Kennel Clubs
Please contact your Kennel Club to obtain contact information about breed clubs in your area.

UK
The Kennel Club (UK)
1 Clarges Street London, W1J 8AB
Telephone: 0870 606 6750
Fax: 0207 518 1058
Web: www.thekennelclub.org.uk

USA
American Kennel Club (AKC)
5580 Centerview Drive, Raleigh, NC 27606.
Telephone: 919 233 9767
Fax: 919 233 3627
Email: info@akc.org
Web: www.akc.org

United Kennel Club (UKC)
100 E Kilgore Rd, Kalamazoo,
MI 49002-5584, USA.
Tel: 269 343 9020
Fax: 269 343 7037
Web: www.ukcdogs.com

Australia
Australian National Kennel Council (ANKC)
The Australian National Kennel Council is the administrative body for pure breed canine affairs in Australia. It does not, however, deal directly with dog exhibitors, breeders or judges. For information pertaining to breeders, clubs or shows, please contact the relevant State or Territory Body.

International
Fédération Cynologique Internationalé (FCI)
Place Albert 1er, 13, B-6530 Thuin, Belgium.
Tel: +32 71 59.12.38
Fax: +32 71 59.22.29
Web: www.fci.be

Training and behavior
UK
Association of Pet Dog Trainers
Telephone: 01285 810811
Web: www.apdt.co.uk

Canine Behaviour
Association of Pet Behaviour Counsellors
Telephone: 01386 751151
Web: www.apbc.org.uk

USA
Association of Pet Dog Trainers
Tel: 1 800 738 3647
Web: www.apdt.com

American College of Veterinary Behaviorists
Web: www.dacvb.org

American Veterinary Society of Animal Behavior
Web: www.avsabonline.org

Australia
APDT Australia Inc
Web: www.apdt.com.au

For details of regional behaviourists, contact the relevant State or Territory Controlling Body.

Activities

UK

Agility Club
Web: www.agilityclub.co.uk

British Flyball Association
Telephone: 01628 829623
Web: www.flyball.org.uk

USA

North American Dog Agility Council
Web: www.nadac.com

North American Flyball Association, Inc.
Tel/Fax: 800 318 6312
Web: www.flyball.org

Australia

Agility Dog Association of Australia
Tel: 0423 138 914
Web: www.adaa.com.au

NADAC Australia
Web: www.nadacaustralia.com

Australian Flyball Association
Tel: 0407 337 939
Web: www.flyball.org.au

International

World Canine Freestyle Organisation
Tel: (718) 332-8336
Web: www.worldcaninefreestyle.org

Health

UK

British Small Animal Veterinary Association
Tel: 01452 726700
Web: www.bsava.com

Royal College of Veterinary Surgeons
Tel: 0207 222 2001
Web: www.rcvs.org.uk

www.dogbooksonline.co.uk/healthcare

Alternative Veterinary Medicine Centre
Tel: 01367 710324
Web: www.alternativevet.org

USA

American Veterinary Medical Association
Tel: 800 248 2862
Web: www.avma.org

American College of Veterinary Surgeons
Tel: 301 916 0200
Toll Free: 877 217 2287
Web: www.acvs.org

Canine Eye Registration Foundation
The Veterinary Medical DataBases
1717 Philo Rd, PO Box 3007,
Urbana, IL 61803-3007
Tel: 217-693-4800
Fax: 217-693-4801
Web: www.vmdb.org/cerf.html

Orthopaedic Foundation of Animals
2300 E Nifong Boulevard
Columbia, Missouri, 65201-3806
Tel: 573 442-0418
Fax: 573 875-5073
Web: www.offa.org

American Holistic Veterinary Medical
Association
Tel: 410 569 0795
Web: www.ahvma.org

Australia

Australian Small Animal Veterinary
Association
Tel: 02 9431 5090
Web: www.asava.com.au

Australian Veterinary Association
Tel: 02 9431 5000
Web: www.ava.com.au

Australian College Veterinary Scientists
Tel: 07 3423 2016
Web: www.acvsc.org.au

Australian Holistic Vets
Web: www.ahv.com.au